THE STRONG
LEADER'S
HAND

6 ESSENTIAL ELEMENTS
EVERY LEADER MUST MASTER

DANIEL
YORK

For information, email Daniel York at dan@firstcause.org

York, Daniel L., 1958-
      The Strong Leader's Hand/Daniel York
      ISBN: 1461131049
      EAN-13: 978-1461131045

  1. Leadership   2. Character   3. Motivation   4. Vision
       5. Attitude   6. Conduct   7. Teamwork

Also By Daniel York:
I Keep Asking
I Pray Also
Something to think about… in Reveration
Lost on Mount Fuji… and other true stories

THE STRONG LEADER'S HAND

CONTENTS

SPECIAL THANKS

Special thanks to Dr. John George for his help in editing. John brought his formidable experience in both leading and studying leadership—invaluable in helping me shape and format the content of this book. His passion for accuracy is inspiring!

DEDICATION

This book is dedicated to the men and women of the United States Army Cadet Command (USACC) and the 104th Division (LT) who tirelessly and effectively train leaders on and off our college campuses to serve our nation in all walks of life.

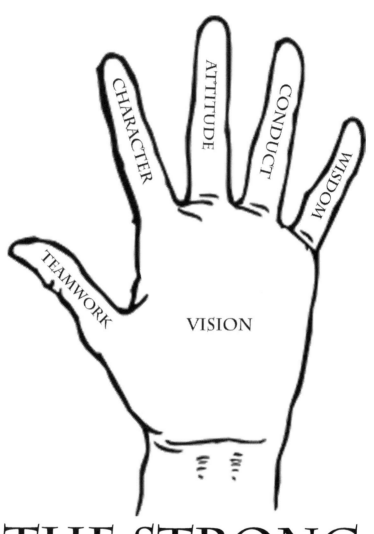

THE STRONG
LEADER'S HAND

"Authority can shape what a person does, but influence shapes who a person becomes."
—Erwin Raphael McManus in *Chasing Daylight*

It was a crisp fall day and the three of us were hungry. I had a *vision* for pizza and as I shared my yearning, my two roommates Bill and Fernando quickly nodded in agreement. Somehow it was decided that I would be the runner. I thought my *character* was sound that day as I set out for Tony's Pizza, that celebrated place where pizzas and calzones came to life below the clock tower. Certainly my *attitude* was positive. I was happy to go and pick up food the three of us craved. Up until that fateful afternoon, my *conduct* at West Point was exemplary. But that would change quickly as I came bolting into Tony's and saw all around me *only* upperclassmen. Slowly heads turned and too many eyes in that room seemed to fasten on me. Something stirred in my brain—that queasy, sick feeling that I was not supposed to be there.

Before I could turn and flee a stern voice addressed me, "Mister, what are you doing here?" No witty reply leaped to my mind for this unknown inquisitor. He asked my name to which I am sure I replied, "Cadet York, Sir!" He asked what company I was in to which I am sure I said, "Sir, Company A-3!" What happened thereafter I cannot recall, except wondering what punishment I would meet. It seemed the *teamwork* of three plebes to combine their money for a pizza was all for naught. Had we taken the time to read our regulations we would have discovered that Tony's was off-limits to fourth classmen.

"What are you doing here?"

The demerits I received were rather light but as word of my escapade spread I became the butt of what seemed every upperclassman's twisted humor for the rest of the year. As I passed by senior cadets in the hallway, I would occasionally catch the snickering, "Hey, York are you going to Tony's today?" It was a question of mirth that tested my mettle. But it also created camaraderie and reminded me to do my best in a place where leaders are forged for a lifetime of service.

West Point prides itself in producing leaders. But leadership is not something merely taught; it must be defined, applied, refined and wisely administered. At the end of this book *we*[1] will share a definition for *leader*, why we chose the descriptor *strong* to describe the leader, why we use the hand as the instrument of illustration, and contrasting styles leaders use. Rather than start with a basic definition, let us look at the essential elements that when mastered make a leader strong and see if we agree on our conclusion!

This book is written primarily for all aspiring leaders who want to improve their leadership skills and, thereby, make a difference in the world. Specifically, we hope that this writing will be a helpful primer to those who will lead in the most unforgiving and exacting of all professions, the military. Through the past three decades of serving in both the military and civilian sector, we have studied many tomes on leadership, observed firsthand great —and not so great—leaders, and sought to master (sometimes well and sometimes poorly) the six elements which I am about to share. These elements when properly understood and applied create strong leaders. Each of the six elements is linked to the hand and layered with true stories so as to make them easier to remember.

By way of disclaimer, I must add that leading is an evolving skill and I am often reminded of how much I have yet to learn. I share many personal observations and convictions in this book with which you may disagree. Please remember my intent is not to gain unanimous consent. My hope is that this book will cause you to think and reflect and in the process become an even better leader!

Before we go through this journey of examining the strong leader, it would be wise to define what a leader is.

Definition of a Leader: A leader is a person people reliably follow to a place they wouldn't normally go.[2]

There are many questions we encourage you to consider as you study this definition.

1. How do we get people to follow us?
2. Why do we qualify the word follow with *reliably*?
3. For what reasons (positive and negative) do people choose to follow leaders?
4. For what reasons do people choose to stop following leaders?
5. Why is it people need a leader to go where they

wouldn't normally go (or do what they normally wouldn't do)?

6. What factors make it hard for a leader to move people to a place they do not want to go?

The question may arise as to why we chose the word *strong* as the key descriptor for the leader. *Strong* by definition will directly apply to every element discussed in this book. Consider the following facets: *especially able, competent, or powerful in a specific field or respect* [vision]; *powerful in influence, authority, resources, or means of prevailing or succeeding* [teamwork]; *of great moral power, firmness, or courage* [character]; *mentally powerful or vigorous* [attitude and wisdom]; and, *moving or acting with force* [conduct][3]. *Strong* should not be construed as heavy in the oppressive sense. Rather, each of the fingers is firmly connected and work together to make a sturdy hand.

How do we get people to follow us?

We discussed different ways to depict or illustrate a *leader* incorporating the six elements. After many great suggestions, I chose to go with the hand because each of the elements is then naturally linked—without any one digit, the hand is impaired. How well we put these six components together determines the *strength* of our grip. Strong leaders connect vision, teamwork, character, attitude, conduct, and wisdom to produce outstanding results. We neglect any component at our peril. As we age and our hands become wrinkled, the more selective we should be about what we do. Not everything we put our hand to is appropriate or successful. Life is a journey—not meant to be rushed or taken for granted. With this in mind, it is time to examine the six essential elements every strong leader must master.

CHAPTER ONE

VISION
The Hand

Vision influences the *direction* and *commitment* of leadership.

Vision is the ability to perceive a desired end state. Strong leaders recognize that vision is essential to move people or groups of people to do what is necessary to achieve success. Vision affects:

<u>who</u> is recruited, educated, and empowered;

<u>what</u> an organization will do;

<u>how</u> it will go about its business;

<u>where</u> an organization will go or remain;

<u>when</u> transformation should occur;

<u>why</u> people should engage in the activities or work they do.

Essentially, vision influences the direction and commitment of leadership.

What you put your hand to, reveals what's important in your life. Let me emphasize again, *what you put your hand to, reveals what's important in your life.* Metaphorically and in actuality what you put your hand to represents your vision. To reach a place of solid leadership, we must understand and embrace vision! Have you ever served a leader without vision? Who pops into your mind? Was serving that leader valuable and good for the organization? Have you ever served a visionary leader? Whose image comes to mind? How did this leader influence the organization?

"Action without vision just passes the time..."

Here is what other leaders have said about the union of vision with leadership.

Rushworth M. Kidder: "Leadership, especially in democratic organizations and nations, is not about tactics, micromanagement, and fine detail. It is about articulating shared values and developing a vision for the future—since that, after all, is how consensus is built and gridlock broken."[4]

Joel Barker: "Vision without action is merely a dream. Action without vision just passes the time. Vision with action can change the world."[5]

Warren G. Bennis: "Leadership is the capacity to translate vision into reality."[6]

George Barna: "A mark of a great leader is the ability not only to capture the vision, but also to articulate it and to cause people to fully embrace it . . . Risk is a natural and unavoidable outgrowth of vision . . . Realize that your vision will reflect your most basic values and beliefs"[7]

There are *four important facets* related to vision. *First, it is crucial we craft a vision that is sound and enduring.*

In March of 2011, when a devastating tsunami wiped out the low-lying communities along Japan's northeastern shore, one hamlet remained quite safe. In the town of Aneyoshi, a single centuries-old tablet was inscribed with the following words: "High dwellings are the peace and harmony of our descendants. Remember the calamity of the great tsunamis. Do not build any homes below this point." Because of their ancestors' vision in understanding danger, the villagers in Aneyoshi built their homes on high ground and were untouched by the great wave.[8]

A significant piece in sustaining a sound and enduring vision is the creation of goals that encompass and wrap the vision so that all who are involved can bring it to fruition. We want to set SMART goals: **S**pecific, **M**easurable, **A**ction Oriented, **R**ealistic (challenging but achievable) and **T**imely (set a specific time for the goal to be completed)

Microsoft's vision for example is "A personal computer in every home running Microsoft software." Notice how simple yet enduring this statement is. Furthermore, it is crafted in such a way that goals may be established to achieve its stated purpose.

Second, (assuming that the vision is appropriate and clearly formulated), *we have to effectively communicate it.* The following story gives us a great example of a helpful example: Cal was interviewing to be the executive director of a nonprofit organization. Along with his resume, he submitted three one page proposals of initiatives he would bring to the organization if they hired him. He was the only candidate to do this and as Ed, the current chairman of the board related, not only did the organization hire Cal, they knew from his initiatives what his focus would be and this led to over fifteen years of successful leadership.

Effective communication requires frequent reinforcing. Fumihiko Imamura, is a professor in disaster planning at Tohoku University in Sendai, the city badly damaged by the 2011 tsunami. He noted that far too many people were killed by the tsunami because they forgot how dangerous it is to live in low-lying areas. He said, "It takes about three generations for people to forget. Those that experience the disaster themselves pass it to their children and their grandchildren, but then the memory fades."[9] Along the coastline of Japan there are many tablets like the one in Aneyoshi. Unfortunately, the vision for keeping people safe was not reinforced and over time disregarded. A forgotten vision is no vision.

> # Effective communication requires frequent reinforcing.

Third, we have to obtain buy-in. Most people naturally resist change. It is not necessarily easy to win the hearts of people to a vision. People oppose change for many reasons. They may be tired. They may lack confidence or trust in their leaders. They may feel unappreciated. So not only is it important to communicate vision clearly, it is also essential to gain the hearts and minds of those we serve so they are willing to be part of our team.

My West Point roommate Dave was selected to lead an organization where many on the staff were advancing in age. Dave recognized that for the organization to grow and be vibrant he needed to bring in new leaders and to recruit new staff. In order to accomplish buy-in, he announced up front that he would serve five years with the intent that he would be replaced by a younger leader. By doing this, he personally modeled the seriousness of his intent. This further increased his credibility in asking older leaders to step aside. As Dr. John George shared, "It has been said 'Your walk talks and your talk talks, but if your walk does not talk louder than your talk talks, nobody pays any attention.'"

The fourth facet regarding vision is that we must hold it with an open hand. Vision does not always turn out the way we planned or hoped. We have to be willing to let our vision adapt and to grow. I grew up with parents that worked for an organization called The Navigators. Eleven of my first eighteen years we lived in Okinawa, Korea, Japan and the Philippines. Consequently, before I left to attend West Point and serve in the military, it was my personal vision to join The Navigators and live and work in Asia. My plans and goals were clear. Have you ever been in a place in life where you were pretty sure you knew what you were going to do?

In 1986 I left the military to join The Navigators. Six months into my training in San Diego, California, all the people who recruited me and were responsible for my training left. I call it the *ministry of abandonment!* The departing leaders moved to their new assignments leaving me with the need to find another source for training.

During the next three years my wife Kathleen and I stayed in San Diego. I enrolled in a local seminary in order to complete a master's degree. Two of our three children were born in La Mesa, California while we continued preparing for what we expected to be a career serving in Asia. Shortly before graduating from seminary, I traveled to Thailand to coordinate a short-term mission trip. My folks lived in Bangkok at the time and after spending a week with them, my dad asked me if I would come over to Southeast Asia and serve as a Navigator leader in one of the nations there. That request was the culmination of my dreams. He was in effect *handing* me my vision.

The night following dad's invitation, I could not sleep. I spent miserable and frustrating hours tossing and turning, knowing that something was wrong. I got up the next morning and told my father that at that point in time I could not say "yes."

I returned home, very unsettled as to what my family should do.

Months later Kathleen and I attended a party at Dana Point in San Diego with a Sunday school class that I was teaching for young married couples in our church. Our two-year old son Bryan was walking robotically on the sand. We took him in for testing and Magnetic Resonance Imaging (MRI) from the neck down, but the results showed no problems. However, within months, Bryan's eyes began to cross. His eye doctor told us to get him to a neurologist immediately!

On Valentine's Day, 1991, Kathleen and I walked into Dr. Schultz's office. The first words out of his mouth were "Mr. and Mrs. York, you need to sit down." I don't know about you, but when I'm told to sit down, the information that follows is never good. So I stayed on my feet. That didn't help. As kindly as possible the troubled doctor told us: "I'm very sorry, I don't really know how to tell you this, but your son has a brain-stem glioma. It is inoperable and fatal. There's nothing we can do. He has *maybe* a five percent chance to survive."

In March and April, I took Bryan to a radiation facility for a total of 72 treatments. Twice a day for 36 days, we drove from our apartment in National City to San Diego, so he could lie still and be zapped. Bryan was so cooperative that he never required anesthesia and the nurses loved him!

Now I have to interrupt this story to ask several pertinent questions. Was my vision to move overseas at this point a realistic vision? No it was not. Who was in control? Not me.

My vision collapsed—it had little chance of succeeding with Bryan's situation. What I thought I was going to be able to do literally dissolved. I remember one Sunday standing in the parking lot of the church we attended crying my guts out. I looked up and said, *"Lord, what is it You're doing? If You want to take our son, it's okay, because You made him. I'll still follow You, and I'll still love You, but what is the point of all this?!? What are we supposed to do?"* I was in the middle of a dark cloud with no idea when the sun would shine again.

"There's nothing we can do."

One of my seminary professors called me in April and told me about a church in Oregon that was looking for a pastor to start a new church. He suggested I put in a resume. I am sure I must have thought, *"Have you forgotten my circumstances! I've never pastored a church in my life, let alone start one. My son is dying! What part of this don't you understand?!*

> **"I had to die to my own vision before I understood His vision for me."**

But, because there was nothing to lose, I did what he asked and mailed out a resume.

Soon thereafter, I received a call from Oregon. The leaders of the church liked my application and wanted to interview me. Unbelievable! In May, I flew up to Oregon to meet with their search committee. I had one of the most relaxed interviews of my life. Essentially, I told them that if they hired me, they were making a mistake. I explained to them my family's situation. The prognosis of Bryan living was bleak. I told them about my shattered vision and the reality that I had absolutely no experience starting a church. (Growing up I used to have friends suggest to me that I should be a pastor and I thought *they* were crazy!) Regardless of my disclaimers, the men interviewing me were friendly and kind. We had a great discussion but I left pretty sure that I'd never hear from them again.

In June I received a phone call. It was from the pastor of the church in Beaverton. Rick said, "Dan we selected you and we want you and your family to move up here and start a church!" Now at that point in time Kathleen and I decided that if they were brave enough to take a chance on me, what were we going to do? How could we say "no"? Only God could set up something this insane and make it work! Rational people don't do things like that. What company in their right mind would have hired me?

Our lives were about to go in a completely different direction. When it comes to vision—hold it with an open hand. If you want your organization or personal life to succeed, be open to the fact that vision may have to change. Life is not static. Circumstances and events often cause us to reevaluate and shift what we think is important. Personally, I entrust my life and the lives of my family to God. I believe His leadership is paramount and that His will is sovereign. I had to die to my own vision before I understood His vision for me. Amazingly, Bryan's brain tumor was miraculously healed. He should have died, but God had other plans for his life as well!

Depending on who or what you believe in will impact your understanding and execution of vision. So be wise and keep an open hand! The question now is, "What will you put your hand to?"

****

Terry de la Mesa Allen (nicknamed "Terrible Terry Allen") was given a colossal challenge. This flamboyant, charismatic leader almost saw his career end after he was relieved of commanding the First Infantry Division in Italy during World War II. Yet, because he was such a fierce fighter who instilled a warrior spirit in his men, the Army's top generals asked him to take command of the 104th Division, known as the Timberwolves.

Major General Allen knew from experience in Africa and Italy that the Germans were ferocious opponents. So he took an innovative approach to training. Before his division shipped to Europe to fight, Allen insisted that his men train at night. At Camp Carson, Colorado, the 104th Division conducted nightly maneuvers and exercises. Finally, the Timberwolves deployed to Europe and advanced through fighting across France, the Netherlands, and Germany. The 104th repulsed several fierce German counterattacks late in 1944 and 1945.

To prevent high numbers of casualties, General Allen often told his men, to put their bullets away, fix bayonets, and pack grenades! They were fighting at night. Then they audaciously attacked without firing their rifles or machine guns. If they heard a weapon go off, they knew it was a German firing at them. Pity the poor soldier who fired his weapon at them! He faced Timberwolves proficient in fighting in the darkness.

The 104th Division fought 195 straight days in combat. No division in the history of the United States ever accomplished such an amazing feat! Because Terry Allen was such an innovative leader countless lives were saved! He understood something precious called VISION. By the end of the war, the 104th Division was considered an elite fighting force winning a reputation as the nation's premier night fighters.[10]

Now let's move forward from World War II to meet a man known as Terrill K. Moffett. TK grew up in Amory, Mississippi, the youngest of nine children living in a home with no running water. Before he left home, three of his brothers died from muscular dystrophy. His father was a carpenter and was often away working. He was also an alcoholic and when he got drunk he often was both mean and violent. Before he returned home from work on Friday nights he went out drinking. Family relatives hid the children in a pasture so their dad would not find and abuse them. When TK was only seven-years old, his father took his own life with a gun in the family living room.

Holding the family together was a very God-fearing mother who did her best to help her children succeed. Amazingly she was not even allowed to drive a car or vote. With her encouragement, TK worked hard in school and in sports motivated to be the best. One year he read thirty-five books and turned in reports for each one—so many the teacher asked him to stop. In the 7th grade he decided he wanted to go to West Point. In the 11th grade, using an old broken typewriter he typed letters to his congressmen expressing his desire to attend the Military Academy. Through his perseverance he received nominations to Annapolis, the Air Force Academy, and West Point.

In 1971, Cadet Moffett graduated from West Point and received his commission as a Second Lieutenant. For five years he served in the active Army and then he joined the Mississippi National Guard. Eventually he was promoted to the rank of Brigadier General and then to Major General along with selection to command the 104th Division.

Those of us who served at the time, will never forget when Major General Moffett came to Fort Vancouver, Washington, and first walked through our headquarters. Pulling all the leaders together, he looked us in the eye and said, "This place is a pigsty! Clean it up!" He could see something that the rest of us could not see. He had fresh eyes. We were used to working there every day. We didn't see the clutter and mess he saw. He quickly got our attention and put us to work cleaning, throwing out trash, painting, and changing the entrance to the headquarters building so it faced the parade field.

General Moffett did not like to spend much time in his office. He preferred to be out in the field where the soldiers trained. He knew that he would learn more about the needs of his command by getting out with the men and women he served. While spending time watching soldiers of First Brigade train, he was approached by some frustrated drill sergeants. At that time they wore on their dress uniforms a unit crest. It was a little blue bird *"The Fighting Marlin."* The 104th drill sergeants were constantly teased by their active duty counterparts every time they wore those birds on their shoulders. Of course that did not go over well with them. General Moffett didn't like it either. So, what did he do? He had his talented aide-de-camp, design a unit crest that reflected the night fighter heritage he learned in reading about General Terry Allen. Two times he submitted the new design for approval and each time was rejected.

Eventually, after careful research, his staff discovered that part of the old crest design traced back to

He saw something the rest of us could not see.

the Crusades. Knowing the Crusades were politically incorrect, TK traveled to the Institute of Heraldry Historical Society and convinced them to support the new design. The Army G1 was the approving authority and fortunately happened to be TK's West Point classmate! The crest was approved. Now the drill sergeants were able to wear a symbol they could take pride in and General Moffett began sharing the Night Fighter legacy. Wherever he went to speak or to present his commander's coin for excellence, he told the story of the Timberwolves spending 195 consecutive days in combat.

Consider what you are going to put Your hand to.

Two men both saw the potential in the organization they served, and through innovative vision, instilled pride, a fighting spirit, and the professionalism that won worldwide recognition. Vision encompasses believing in your calling and knowing what your mission is. Make sure you carefully consider what you are going to put your hand to and communicate clearly with those who follow you so they know the direction you are headed and the priorities that will make your journey successful.

CHAPTER TWO

TEAMWORK
The Thumb

Teamwork influences the
magnitude of leadership

T he thumb (teamwork) as it overlaps the other fingers in gripping, is a good reminder that we need each other. Perhaps this is even more fittingly illustrated by the handshake. A leader may have all the tools to be effective but always we must remember that we need the cooperation of people to succeed. It is the agreement between leaders and followers to work together and to trust each other that makes organizations safe, resilient, and prosperous.

Teamwork is the joint effort of a group of persons committed to the success of a shared cause. As such it influences the magnitude or extent of leadership. It is a beautiful thing to watch people unite around a common goal to achieve something valuable. But as sure as the big heat tab in the sky will sink in the west, there will always be challenges to teamwork. The earth does not lack for cantankerous, selfish, and mean-spirited people. Nor does everyone have the same views, strengths or energy to contribute.

Patrick Lencioni in his book *The Five Dysfunctions of a Team*, shares valuable insight strong leaders must harness if they are to successfully lead teams. *First, leaders must lead in modeling vulnerability.* As noted earlier, humility and the willingness to learn are two vital attributes of effective leaders. Leaders who are vulnerable are particularly skillful in ridding their teams of an absence of trust, a condition which can paralyze an organization.

Second, strong leaders overcome team members fear of conflict by demonstrating the ability to both allow for disagreement and to teach their subordinates or peers that decision-making is actually improved be inviting dissenting views. Artificial harmony actually stifles creativity and productive ideological conflict.

Third, strong leaders erase a lack of commitment by team members by holding to goals and established standards. An often overlooked aspect of maintaining standards is the practice of conducting rehearsals. Before making presentations, or conducting drills, or engaging in activity that is critical to the organization, rehearse which steps need to be taken, who is responsible for each step, and what behavior or action is essential to meet the established goals and standards.

Fourth, strong leaders tackle head first difficult issues. They do not tolerate team members who deliberately damage the organization by their unethical or inappropriate attitude and behavior. They will take the appropriate measures to counsel and, if necessary, fire disruptive employees. In every war soldiers are removed from duty because they are malingers, thieves, or cowards. It is no different in peacetime. Organizations are comprised of people and not every person is a good employee. The danger for many leaders is that they are wary of creating conflict. Often teams suffer because the boss is not willing to do the hard work of removing disruptive workers. Conflict avoidance is the easy course and usually the wrong course. Passing on "problem employees" to other organizations instead of just firing them is a cowardly technique that just ensures other people

> **Conflict avoidance is usually the wrong course.**

on other teams will suffer. Failing to correct wrong behavior actually can embolden the offender and make the work environment an unsafe place. Teamwork is best accomplished when each team member is made accountable for his or her behavior and belongs and serves according to the needs and mandate of the organization.

Fifth, strong leaders "focus on collective outcomes." Rather than let each team member pursue personal goals or status, the wise leader directs the focus of each member towards the overall objective.[11] However, to get to a collective outcome, strong leaders also focus on the strengths and not the weaknesses of their valued members. Unfortunately, too many leaders assume that the best way to help their team is to correct the weaknesses or failings of their subordinates. This causes unnecessary stress and promotes conflict. No one wants to look bad, or fail, or get pounded for personal weaknesses. Nor does making a person a "project" so as to "fix" him or her often work. Wise leaders learn as much as they can about their teammates and then focus on their strengths. This motivates each person to do even better and allows them to be recognized for what they do well.

We add a sixth component which is that *strong leaders work hard at building and sustaining solid relationships.* Too often leaders focus on work and productivity and miss the underlying need to establish meaningful relationships with their subordinates, peers, and superiors. If people suspect that they are merely a "means to an end", resentment is sure to grow. Here are two examples that illustrate this:

Every week (almost without exception) we receive newsletters in the mail from people we know in nonprofit organizations seeking money. When I look at who the sender is, I make an immediate decision. If that person has never taken the time to call or write us to see how we our doing (relationship building), I throw the letter in the trash. Conversely, if we know the sender to be a friend who has made the effort to invest in our lives, Kathleen and I are eager to read the letter and give to whatever the expressed need is.

My wife and I visited an organization for the first time and we were greeted soon after arriving by a couple that was very friendly. They spent considerable time chatting with us and we were quite taken by their warmth. Just before it was time for us to leave, they revealed that they were involved with a multilevel marketing business and asked if we would be interested in their sharing it with us. Immediately we understood why they were so friendly. Now if this seems judgmental on our part, consider that after we politely declined, from that day forward when we returned they paid us no attention.

Strong leaders do not "use" people, they invest in them. Relational building does not mean that a leader must be "buddies" with everyone. Truly familiarity can breed contempt. However, by *investment* what is meant is that the leader takes and makes the time to know those with whom he or she works. Leaders, who demonstrate that they truly know as much as they can about their teammates and care about them, create a legacy of success.

As leaders it is our responsibility to value those we work with and to ensure that we provide them with the tools they need to succeed. Thus we must differentiate between knowing what is bad and must be removed from what is a weakness and must be overlooked. The better we know our people, the better we will be able to harness their skills and bypass their shortcomings. SFC Luther Tookes pulled me aside as a young lieutenant and told me that the key to successfully leading the platoon was to get to know each and every one of my soldiers. As I watched him at work each day it was obvious he practiced what he preached. Since then I have worked hard to become familiar with the people that I serve. It is surprising what we can learn when we take the time to get to know our teammates. Well functioning teams are so smooth that often it is easy to overlook the hard work and effort that were expended to grow each person to succeed.

Basketball coach Mike Krzyzewski stated, "To me, teamwork is the beauty of our sport, where you have five acting as one. You become selfless."[12] Perhaps the most famous professional football coach, Vince Lombardi shared, "Teamwork is what the Green Bay Packers were all about. They didn't do it for individual glory. They did it because they loved one another."[13] This truth was again displayed in 2011 when Green Bay defeated the Pittsburgh Steelers to win Super Bowl XLV. Despite suffering an inconceivable number of injuries throughout the season and entering the playoffs as a sixth-seeded wild card, Green Bay somehow managed to defeat Philadelphia, Atlanta, and Chicago in their stadiums! By the end of the first half in the championship game, they lost two of their key starters—Charles Woodson on defense and Donald Driver on offense. Without hesitation, their replacements stepped up and filled their roles such that the team prevailed in the second half. The Packers gave us all a living testimony to what can happen when each person understands their role and does their best.

> **They did it because they loved one another.**

There is a Kenyan proverb that states: "A single thumb cannot kill a louse." The meaning is this: Teamwork is very important. Are you making the people around you better? Are you able to work with others? Do you let your teammates take the credit for success and build them up? Or is life all about you?

****

My sister Barbie is a wife and mother to four children. She is the quintessential "fun mom." Often her home is filled with kids from up the street who came over to skateboard, jump on the trampoline, or just hang out with her children. Barbie works the night shift at Meridian Park Hospital. While on duty one night, a patient's blood pressure dropped dangerously low. Barbie called the doctor and shared the sick man's vitals and the doctor said, "You are overreacting just give him fluids." But the man was clammy, pale, and retaining fluids. She knew his condition was deteriorating so she called a *rapid response* which means within minutes a supervisor, respiratory therapist, pharmacist, ICU nurse, and the head nurse all arrived. Like me, you might wonder why in the world five people were needed for a drop in blood pressure.

So Barbie explained to me:

—the supervisor checks the overall condition of the patient

—the respiratory therapist administers oxygen

—the pharmacist ensures the amount of drugs dispensed are proper

—the ICU nurse gives the drugs

—the head nurse helps wherever needed

Most hospitals in the world may not have the ability to assemble a rapid response team but the fact that this hospital can is important. Each of those five persons has a key role. With five sets of eyes, the possibility of identifying the cause of the problem and prescribing the right solution improves dramatically. The team works together to ensure a safe solution is implemented.

****

Have you ever heard of Ranger School? Ranger School is the toughest school the Army has to train its soldiers short of actual combat. If you are in the infantry, you need to go where it's toughest. You want to be molded through fire. Fresh out of West Point, and after completing Officer Basic Training, I volunteered for Ranger School. In November of 1981, Class 2-82 began. We had to go through three phases consisting of training at Fort Benning, the mountains of Dahlonega, Georgia and swamps in Camp Rudder, Florida. The training lasted about two months.

Somehow I injured my Achilles tendon and when we got to the mountain phase in Dahlonega, it became very painful just to walk. At many points the pain was so bad I seriously wondered if I could make it. One of my ranger buddies had personal experience in gutting it out through pain. Often as if he could sense my mood, he would get right behind me on patrols and quietly say things like, "Don't you even think about quitting! Suck it up, you can make it." His consistent encouragement was all I needed to keep going. One morning as we prepared to patrol on a particularly steep area, our ranger instructor (RI) told us not to put our field jackets on because even though the cold air was dense, after we hiked we would start sweating and that would cause us to get wet and potentially suffer hypothermia when the temperature dropped.

Now, I weighed probably 120 pounds. I am sure I was the lightest ranger in that class. I had virtually no body fat and I was cold! I remember thinking, "*To heck with you RI! I'm cold! I'm putting my field jacket on!*" So I wore my coat, and off we went up hills steep enough to make great ski slopes. I focused more on the pain in my tendon and did not

If I didn't tell the RI, I would freeze and potentially die.

think much about the fact that I was quickly warming up. Before long, I began to sweat and I had to take off my field jacket.

Hours later when we set up our patrol base the temperature dropped below freezing and sure enough I started shaking. I could not get warm and I knew I was experiencing the onset of hypothermia. Now I had a choice to make. If I alerted the RI to my condition, he would have to order us to make a fire, which would compromise our security, and cause the patrol leader to fail his graded mission. If I didn't tell the RI it was probable I would freeze and potentially die.

Knowing the risk, I chose not to say anything and hope that somehow I could make it through the night. Mark Cole, a member of the Second Ranger Battalion from Fort Lewis, and also part of our squad of ranger candidates, saw what was happening with me. He came over to me and took his poncho and liner (all we had for warmth), and placed them over my poncho and liner and then laid on top of me until I got warm and was out of danger.

I'm pretty sure Ranger Cole was cold. He was not the patrol leader that night and he did not have to help me. But he was my ranger buddy and ranger buddies take care of each other at all costs. As if that was not amazing enough, Mark did something else I will never forget all of my life.

Throughout our training everyone sooner or later was assigned to carry a machine gun or a radio. Now remember, I didn't weigh much so having to carry a machine gun (M60) or a radio (AN/PRC77) each of which weighed about 20 pounds, along with a rucksack, ammunition, and water meant I was exhausted. In mountainous or swampy terrain, extra weight made it very difficult for me to keep up with a patrol. In the swamps it was already hard to keep our balance because of the vines under the water we called, "wait-a-minute vines." However, each time I was assigned to carry the M60 or the AN/PRC 77, as I would strap them on, Mark would ask me what I was doing. He would give me that look like, "What are you crazy!" He insisted I give him the equipment and he carried it for me. In my eyes he was not just a big guy, he was a man with a giant heart.

I gained ten pounds in winter Ranger School. I think I am probably the only person in the history of the Rangers to *gain* weight—I had to just to survive. When I look at that coveted ranger tab, I remember that if it were not for my ranger buddies, I would never have graduated. It took selfless team-work.

****

Great organizations have a history of unbroken teamwork and special bonding. Each Labor Day weekend, the 104th WWII veterans, widows of veterans and family members called "pups," gather in a city they select and spend several days sightseeing, reminiscing over war memories and catching up on the latest news. One of the greatest days of my life was the day I was promoted to Brigadier General in a large ballroom with these veterans whom I have come to love as family.

One of these vets lives near my home in Oregon and we have had many special times to talk and swap stories. I've noticed that whenever this humble, white-haired man walks into a room his presence is immediately felt and it is obvious how much he is respected. Art Sorenson was captured by the Germans in World War II and yet somehow managed to escape. While serving in the 104th Division, he received the Purple Heart from a combat wound. So gallant was he as a warrior, he was awarded the Silver Star and two Bronze Stars. One of the main reasons Art is alive is because of teamwork. He recalls the time the Third Armor Division needed to advance from the Ramagen Bridge to Nordhausen. They could not advance without infantry support. So Art and his buddies in I, K, and L companies of the 3rd/414th Battalion put as many as ten men on a tank and rode with them forward. Much of their advances were made at night. Whenever they were attacked, the infantry dismounted and counterattacked to prevent the Germans from disabling their tanks with antitank missiles. On Easter day, Art remembers advancing into a valley where they were ambushed and promptly lost six tanks. But again, because the infantry worked with the armor, ultimately, they were able to push the Germans back and win the war. Those tanks helped keep the infantrymen alive and vice versa.

Art and his wife Bette, Mel, Dick and Virginia, Glen and Marilyn, and countless fallen heroes represent a time in our nation where everyone rolled up their sleeves, made tough sacrifices, and, by uncommon determination, freed the world of two empires bent on conquest. The freedoms we too often take for granted were purchased through teamwork. But it was not easy.

Today we live in a world where freedom is assaulted by those who would inflict their terror at any time and any place. Terrorists would impose their misguided and corrupt ideology on any and all who oppose them. While the face of the enemy constantly changes, as well as the techniques utilized to inflict harm, the need for teamwork is just as necessary. Those who are vigilant and who work well together will always have an advantage!

CHAPTER THREE

CHARACTER
The Index Finger

Character influences the *nature* and *quality* of leadership.

C haracter is the summative features, quali-
ties, and traits that form one's nature and
reputation. Character is about our *being*.
Character influences the nature and quality
of leadership because it builds trust, the
essential foundation of a leader's relationship with
those led. Character is built around what we value
and hold dearly. Before he died, Captain Donald
Hiebert wrote a statement that reflects a clear understanding of values. Donny was an Air Force
Academy graduate who died in a B-52G plane crash
while on a training mission April 11, 1983. He
wrote:

I only want to raise a family, serve my fellow man (mostly young people), give credence to the Gospels, strive for holiness, and be a gentle soul. I'd rather teach philosophy than poli-sci, fly a kite than a B-52, lead my family in prayer than men into battle. And yet, this profession means so much to me.[14]

Secretary of Defense, Robert Gates and senior Army leaders are concerned that after ten straight years of combat it is important to clearly define the military profession. Much of a white paper written to stimulate soldier's input about their profession was concerned with ethics and morality. The reason for this is clear. An ever present concern for the military is to establish and protect trust with the public it is sworn to defend. *Trust is an essential part of character.* In order for leaders to be trusted, they must be people of noble disposition. For this reason, officers and noncommissioned officers are expected to personally embrace and teach their soldiers seven values which establish character worthy of trust: loyalty, duty, respect, selfless service, honor, integrity and personal courage.

Read what influential people from the past have written or said about character:

Aristotle: "Character may almost be called the most effective means of persuasion."[15]

George Washington: "I hope I shall possess firmness and virtue enough to maintain what I consider the most enviable of all titles: the character of an honest man."[16]

Abraham Lincoln: "Character is like a tree, and reputation is like a shadow.. The shadow is what we think of it. The tree is the real thing."[17]

Helen Keller: "Character cannot be developed in ease and quiet. Only through experience of trial and suffering can the soul be strengthened, vision cleared, ambition inspired, and success achieved."[18]

> "When character is lost, all is lost."

Billy Graham: "When wealth is lost, nothing is lost. When health is lost, something is lost. When character is lost, all is lost."[19]

West Point once had a mission statement that read: "It is the purpose of the United States Military Academy to provide the nation with leaders of character." In truth, it ought to be the mission of every institution to provide the nation with leaders of character. When a nation loses its moral compass, we can be sure its descent into destruction will be swift.

In his book *How Good People Make Tough Choices*, Rushworth Kidder writes that character is more than just what you are in the dark. Character has a social as well as a personal aspect. "First it's what you let others know you to be—the way you communicate to others an openness to ethical concern, a willingness to engage tough moral issues, an invitation to challenge your actions by your values."[20]

He goes on to write:

Second, ethical fitness doesn't exist in a personal vacuum. Show me the person of solid character who doesn't have a single ethical colleague and I'll show you a person who is either so inspired as to be a saint or so out of touch with reality as to be delusional. Like coals in a fireplace, we keep ourselves ethically fit by contact with each other. Set any one of us alone on the moral hearth, and we're apt to turn into a cold, dark cinder.[21]

Ethical fitness benefits mightily in the right organizational culture. Where people band together to do what is right under the approval of an organization, good things are bound to happen. Conversely, if an immoral culture pervades an environment, there will be continuous pull on those of strong character to compromise their convictions.[22]

> **It is essential we recognize that character is reflected in our being.**

It is essential we recognize that character is reflected in our *being*. So much of our culture is caught up in *doing*. Jim Loehr and Tony Schwartz wrote in *The Power of Full Engagement*, "Without time for recovery, our lives become a blur of *doing* unbalanced by much opportunity for *being*." Fatigue, stress, and temptation can and will wear down self-control. It is not just moral compromise or surrounding ourselves with dissolute (immoral) people that can create fissures in our character. Constant, frenetic activity wears down our will to be morally resolute. Strong character requires ethical fitness. It is rare today to find leaders who emphasize the importance of rest! Yet the reality is that any organization whose leaders do not personally rest or teach their people to find respite and relax will inexorably

Do you make time to replenish your energy; time to renew your convictions?

wear itself out!

"Psychologists have discovered that self-control is an exhaustible resource."[23]

Most of us until faced with major disease or physical breakdown tend to be hard on our bodies. Consequently, in our tired state, we may fail to see the effects on our character. It is often when we are forced to slow down that we understand just how much our life and our character matter. My friend and classmate Dan, following a major heart attack, wears a defibrillator in his heart. For Dan rest is not an option, it is lifesaving. Recently when I emailed him and asked how his body was holding up, he responded:

> The body is tired most often. I am taking naps on a regular basis just because there is no gas available. I must believe that God gives me the strength to do those things He would have me do. I will continue to live until He decides that I have had all the breaths that I should have. And then I will behold those

things (that One) that would take my breath away.[24]

Who are your friends? What types of people surround you? What's your nature like? Do you hold to high standards or would you rather swim in the pond of decadence? Do you make the time to replenish your energy and renew your convictions? We have to protect our character. As soon as we begin to rationalize behavior that is wrong or to compromise our integrity, we set ourselves up for failure. Without sound character, a leader's vision may never come to fruition and his or her hand is arthritic at best.

****

I learned about character growing up watching and listening to my father. First he taught my two sisters, brother, and me that there were three things we were not to do or we would immediately incur punishment. We had better not lie, steal, or treat people disrespectfully. Growing up was more than just following rules, it was also learning to be honorable. I remember two occasions in high school where dad after traveling to Malaysia shared stories with us in our home in the Philippines. On one occasion he went jogging down a beach in Penang when a woman dressed in red began chasing him.

She wasn't able to catch him but while he ran it was apparent in his mind that what she was after could only get him in trouble. On another trip late at night, he received a call in his hotel room from a man asking if he would like a woman. Alone and in a place where no one would have known, it would have been easy to compromise and do what he knew was wrong. Instead he resisted and kept morally pure.

****

Early in the 1980s I had the privilege of serving as the first aide-de-camp to Brigadier General Parker. BG Parker was like a father to me in many ways. He did not perform just his job as the Assistant Division Commander of Operations, he consistently took the time throughout our days together to share observations and lessons that helped professionally develop me as a lieutenant. I called Lieutenant General (retired) Parker to ask him to share with us his thoughts on character. This is the story he shared.:

While serving as the Commandant of the Aviation School at Fort Rucker, Alabama, allegations were raised that two officers in the aviation course cheated. There was enough circumstantial evidence for General Parker to conduct an Article

32 investigation. The investigation concluded that the two officers had cheated but there was not enough evidence to convict them in court. So Parker decided to interview the two men separately on his own. One of the officers attended his church, and two respected members of the congregation (one was an attorney) asked if they could sit in when the General conducted his interview. Convinced that he was innocent, they wanted to serve as character witnesses for the young man. Parker agreed to let them join him.

When the first officer reported to him, the General read him his rights then said, "Think long and hard before you answer my questions. Cheating is bad but it

The men walked out stunned, their heads down.

is more forgivable than lying. If you lie to me it means you have a character flaw." The young man answered his questions and denied having cheated. The next officer came in and was similarly questioned. He, too, denied any wrongdoing. But in the course of the interview, he presented new information. General Parker then called back the first officer and by carefully using the new information, the man questioned broke down and began crying. He confessed to cheating in his aviation course. In clearing his conscience, he shared that he had also broken the Honor Code of the Military Academy and he felt great remorse for his actions. The two men from his church were stunned and walked out of the room with their heads down.

The next officer came in again and when he learned of the other's confession, he, too, finally admitted to lying and cheating. In lieu of a court martial, General Parker asked for both of their resignations from the Army. He then took the extra measure of writing both of their parents to explain what he had done and why. One of the mothers was angry with him and wrote him several letters that expressed her displeasure in the actions General Parker took. She shared that children often cheat in school and get away with it. He replied and explained to her that the military is the one profession which is charged with training people to make decisions which often involve sending young men and women into harm's way. He was training officers to lead men in combat and that he had young sons

> **A leader who lies has a price for integrity. He will lie when the price is met.**

himself. "I take integrity seriously. In combat, the one thing I want to know is that a leader has no price for his honesty/integrity." He often shared with his sons while they were growing up, "When in doubt, always do what is right!"

General Parker went on to share with her that a leader who lies, demonstrates that he has a price for integrity and will lie whenever that price is met. Such a leader cannot be trusted when lives are on the line in combat. Conversely, there is great security and confidence in the soldier or employee who can trust his or her leader because the leader's character is sound. As the mother read Parker's words, she took them to her pastor and he helped her see the wisdom and truth in what the General shared with her. She made peace with him and wrote that she wished her son would have had leaders like him in high school.

****

My deputy, Gail, lost her husband to a rapid bout of lung cancer. What made the loss particularly grievous was that he was in great physical condition, a retired Air Force fighter pilot who did not smoke and was not overweight. Bill was a man of impeccable integrity. On his desk was the following quote: "You can tell the character of a man by the way he treats those who can do nothing for him or to him."

One July day in Chesterfield, VA at a local airfield, Gail and Bill had just completed a flying lesson. They were dating at the time and Bill still had four other students that hot afternoon. When he finished giving his last lesson, he came into the pilot lounge to get her. Gail gave him a cold Coke and they sat down to discuss how she did with the new aerobatic maneuvers he taught her. Bill paused for a moment and took a small note pad from his sweaty pocket. He then asked if she had a pen. She did and after giving it to him watched as he opened the sweaty pages of his old note book and begin to write. When he was done a few minutes later, he put the note pad back in the front pocket of his shirt.

"Bill, what are you writing in your note pad?" He answered, "Oh, I'm just recording each of the ten-dollar bills I received from the students today. He wrote the date, amount, and name of each student. Since they were dating, he wouldn't let Gail pay him $10. She then asked him why he did this. He replied, "So I can record the exact amount of money I earn from teaching flying on my tax forms." She was so impressed by his sincerity, integrity, honesty and character, that it brought tears to her eyes. She remembers telling him, "Bill, I am so proud to be with you today." He smiled his usual humble smile and then proceeded to critique her lesson.

The reason I share this story is that too often we relate character to big issues when in reality it is the little things that can make or break us. If we do what we know in our conscience to be wrong by breaking laws that seem insignificant or stretching the truth with others, then we are headed towards much bigger compromises and ethical breaches. Once our character is cracked we are far more susceptible to ruin.

****

Effectual character is persevering. It is not some wind-shifted trait that vanishes and appears based on external circumstances. Anne models this truth. The oldest of ten children, I learned about Anne through her sister Theresa, one of my West Point classmates. Anne was a teacher in Guatemala and after working many years on staff in different schools she decided to start a Christian school. Frustrated in not being able to obtain a facility to use, she converted her own home into a place to teach many underprivileged and needy children. Later in life, she became a school teacher in California. Despite poor health, due to post polio syndrome, Anne works hard to teach children—and not just in the classroom.

Anne became concerned that the town in which she worked, Santa Ana, did not celebrate the Fourth of July. So she worked hard organizing volunteers so that this omission was corrected. For three straight years, Santa Ana celebrated Independence Day. More importantly her school children learned about the value of our freedom and our nation's heritage. In 2010 a Hispanic man, who did not like the fact that the city was now recognizing and celebrating the Fourth of July, opposed Anne's work. Through a dishonest video interview in which he selectively edited content, he attempted to make the organizers appear racist. By threatening to mount a protest, this individual successfully intimidated the City Council to postpone awarding a certificate of recognition for Anne's group. Furthermore she was accused of being part of a "hate group."

Rather than back down, Anne personally addressed the City Council and chastised them for not investigating the facts behind the charges of racism. Instead of caving in to the pressure of a man with a misguided agenda who did not represent the views of most citizens, she boldly held to her convictions. Along with her many supporters she pledged to continue working to ensure the city could celebrate an important holiday. Along the way she modeled for her class the value of holding fast to one's core values.

CHAPTER FOUR

ATTITUDE
The Middle Finger

Attitude influences the *spirit, will* and *force* of leadership

"He was my gunny, sir.. He was a really good man. He was my hero—not just for the way he died, but for the way he lived."—Lance Corporal Mejia[25]

A ttitude is the mental and emotional view and mood applied to people, things, or circumstances. Brian Tracy stated, "Your attitude is an expression of your values, beliefs and expectations." Attitude is the fuel. It influences the spirit, will, and force of leadership. Without the right attitude, leaders can both fail to inspire others and personally succumb to the challenges life offers. Internally, strong leaders strive to do their best, adaptive to change, resilient to adversity. Externally, strong leaders convey a positive, can-do spirit to encourage and inspire.

Humility is a key virtue when it comes to attitude. Humble leaders breed trust and create a place that is safe for employees to grow and work. Conversely, leaders who always have to be right and who demonstrate an attitude of superiority alienate their employees and create resentment. John Ruskin said, "I believe the first test of a truly great man is in his humility."[26]

Conversely, leaders who always have to be right and who demonstrate an attitude of superiority alienate their employees and create resentment. We have learned from many leaders what not to do but we have grown most under humble leaders.

Humor is a wonderful technique for dissolving bad attitudes. Many times an atmosphere permeated by fear, sarcasm, paranoia, anger, critical words or ill will can be reduced enormously by leaders who are able to initiate wit or comedy that breaks the tension. Strong leaders have enough backbone and fiber to know when it is wise to poke fun of themselves in order to raise the spirits of those around them. Similarly they know what persons can be called upon to inject humor when spirits are low.

Often there is humor to be found in many situations. I will never forget the time my family was out fishing and my dad was using a fly rod. As he was casting the line and whipping it back he accidently embedded the hook in his chin. We were all stunned and concerned at his predicament. Instead of getting mad or copping a bad attitude, he joked about it and what was a somewhat tense situation turned into a funny incident.

Earlier we noted that rest is an important component to protecting our character. In a similar manner, exercise is vital in helping our state of mind. Physically, we find that the better our bodies are conditioned because of exercise the stronger and healthier our attitudes are. If we do not get enough sleep and do not run regularly or work out, it is easier to become critical towards people and projects. Keeping our bodies in shape involves eating the right food, resting properly and exercising. Personally, I find that if I run three times a week and on days when I am not running take my dogs out for a vigorous walk, my blood pressure is healthy, I *feel* strong, and I

Show me a hero; I'll show you an extra- ordinary attitude.

generally have an upbeat, positive attitude. Strong leaders recognize the need for physical exercise and work hard to create good habits that will keep them fit for life!

General George C. Marshall was arguably one of the greatest leaders in U.S. history. Despite his amazing organizational skills, it was his attitude that helped propel his success. Marshall writing to a VMI professor in 1920 counseled:

> When conditions are difficult, the command is depressed, and everyone seems critical and pessimistic, you must be especially cheerful and optimistic... The more alarming and disquieting the reports received or the conditions viewed in battle, the more determined must be your attitude.[27]

Pastor and author Chuck Swindoll testified, "The longer I live, the more convinced I become that life is 10% what happens to us and 90% how we respond to it."[28]

Coach Vince Lombardi said, "If you aren't fired with enthusiasm, you will be fired with enthusiasm."[29]

F. Scott Fitzgerald wrote, "Show me a hero and I will write you a tragedy."[30] Show us a hero and we will show you an extraordinary attitude!

****

In 1985 I deployed as part of Task Force 3/502nd Battalion to the Sinai. Our assignment was to man observation points scattered throughout the desert so as to keep the peace between Egypt and Israel. Our Battalion Commander was concerned about our soldiers accidentally discharging their weapons so he gave an order that we were to duct tape our magazines to prevent a round from chambering in our M16s. It was an unwise order for two reasons. First, rather than treat us like responsible adults and expect us to properly handle our weapons this was a safety move that showed a lack of trust in our ability to handle weapons. Second, his order actually served to put us in greater danger. Had any terrorist attacked our observation points our soldiers stood a great chance of dying. By the time they got the duct tape off their magazine and loaded their weapons, it would have been too late to defend against a serious attack.

The attitude of our commander during our time in the desert consistently was to ensure that no incidents took place that might tarnish our record or cause us as a unit to be embarrassed. Unfortunately, it had an unintended effect—it caused many of us to question whether the boss was really most interested in our safety or in his own reputation.

On December 12, 1985, this same commander and 247 other peacekeepers perished when the plane they were flying home crashed in Gander, Newfoundland. This was the single most tragic accident the 101st Airborne Division (Air Assault) ever suffered. Controversy still swirls over what caused the crash of that Arrow Airline plane. But three things are certain: While the plane sat in Cairo, Egypt and refueled, no guards were posted which gave opportunity to unauthorized people to access that aircraft. Second, the plane was carrying too much weight. Third, the airlines the government contracted to fly us had previous maintenance problems and soldiers actually expressed concerns to their loved ones prior to returning home, about the safety of the jet.

If our commander was aware of the poor maintenance record of Arrow Airlines and the concerns of his soldiers of flying on their aircraft, he did not notify his chain of command and warn them of the dangers. Nor did he ensure that the proper security and safeguards were taken to guard the aircraft which was loaded with weapons. While it would not be expected that he would know the plane was overweight, his failure to take safety seriously resulted in tremendous loss of life to include his own. Why would a man so concerned about a weapon going off accidentally not show an intense concern over the travel of almost 1/3rd of his task force. I believe in some ways, his attitude was the underlying problem as well as an over heightened concern for his own career (which could be considered a serious character flaw). Not only did he lack the warrior ethos that commands respect and instills pride, his mind-set consistently revealed a preoccupation with satiating his own needs. In the end, lives that might have been saved were needlessly lost. The tragedy of Gander was that a commander who should have been diligent didn't care.

****

I asked my West Point classmate and good friend Greg, who is a business coach, if he would share a positive example of the importance of attitude. Greg sent the following story:[31]

On Nov 13, 2010, Marine Lieutenant General John Kelly gave a speech to the Semper Fi Society of St. Louis. This was four days after his son, Lt. Robert Kelly, USMC was killed by an improvised explosive device (IED) while on his third combat tour. General Kelly spoke about the dedication and valor of the young men and women who step forward each and every day to protect us. Not once did the grieving father mention the loss of his own son. He closed his message with the moving account of the last 6 seconds in the lives of two young Marines who died with rifles blazing to protect their brother Marines.

On April 22, 2008, two Marine infantry battalions, 1/9 "The Walking Dead," and 2/8 were switching out in Ramadi with one battalion going stateside while the other was just starting its seven-month combat tour. Representing each battalion, Corporal Jonathan Yale and Lance Corporal Jordan Haerter, 22 and 20 years old respectively, assumed the watch together at the entrance gate of an outpost that contained a makeshift barracks housing 50 Marines. The same ramshackle building was also home to 100 Iraqi police; allies in the fight against the Al Qaeda in a city that once held distinction as the most dangerous metropolis on earth.

Corporal Yale grew up a dirt poor, mixed-race kid from Virginia. Back home he supported a wife, daughter, mother and sister who together lived under one roof. He did this on a yearly salary of less than $23,000. Lance Corporal Haerter in contrast, was a middle class young man from Long Island. These two soldiers, forged in the same crucible of training, were brothers as close, or closer, than if they were born of the same woman.

The mission orders they received from the sergeant squad leader probably went something like: "Okay you two clowns, stand this post and let no unauthorized personnel or vehicles pass. You clear?" In all likelihood Yale and Haerter rolled their eyes and said in unison something like: "Yes Sergeant," with just enough attitude that made the point without saying the words, "No kidding sweetheart, we know what we're doing." They then relieved two other Marines on watch and took up their post at the entry control point of Joint Security Station Nasser, in the Sophia section of Ramadi, Al Anbar, Iraq.

A few minutes later a large blue truck turned down the alley way, perhaps 60-70 yards in length, and sped its way through the serpentine of concrete jersey walls. The truck stopped just short of where the two were posted and detonated, killing them both catastrophically. Twenty-four brick masonry houses were damaged or destroyed. A mosque 100 yards away collapsed. The truck's engine came to rest two hundred yards away knocking most of a house down before it stopped. Explosive experts reckoned the blast was made of 2,000 pounds of explosives. Yet, because these two young infantrymen didn't have it in their DNA to run from danger, they saved 150 of their Iraqi and American brothers-in-arms.

There were no American witnesses to the event, just Iraqi police. General Kelly concluded if there was any chance of finding out what actually happened so he could decorate the two Marines and acknowledge their bravery, he would have to investigate and submit a request above his signature. So he traveled to Ramadi and spoke individually to a half-dozen Iraqi police all of whom told the same story. They said, "We knew immediately what was going on as soon as the two Marines began firing." Some of them also fired, and then to a man, ran for safety just prior to the explosion. All of them survived. Many were injured, some seriously. One of the Iraqis with tears welling up confided that they fled like any normal men would to save their lives. "What he didn't know until then," he said, "and what he learned that very instant, was that Marines are not normal." Choking past the emotion he said, "Sir, in the name of God no sane man would have stood there and done what they did. No sane man. They saved us all."

What General Kelly didn't know at the time, and only learned a couple of days later after he wrote a summary and submitted both Yale and Haerter for posthumous Navy Crosses, was that one of the security cameras, damaged initially in the blast, recorded some of the suicide attack. It happened exactly as the Iraqis described it. It took exactly six seconds from when the truck entered the alley until it detonated.

Putting himself in their heads the general supposed it took about a second for the two Marines to separately come to the same conclusion about what was going on once the truck came into their view at the far end of the alley. With no time to talk it over, or call the sergeant to ask what they should do, they could only know their orders to let no unauthorized vehicle through. The two Marines had about five seconds left to live.

They had five seconds to live...

It took maybe another two seconds for them to raise their weapons, take aim, and fire. By this time the truck was half-way through the barriers and gaining speed. Here, the recording showed a number of Iraqi police, some of whom had fired their rifles, now scattering—some running right past the Marines who had three seconds left to live.

For two seconds more, the recording shows the Marines' weapons firing non-stop. The truck's windshield exploded into shards of glass as their rounds took it apart and as the General recounted, "tore into the body of the SOB who is trying to get past them to kill their brothers, American and Iraqi, bedded down in the barracks totally unaware of the fact that their lives at that moment depended entirely on two Marines standing their ground."

The recording shows the truck careened to a stop immediately in front of the two Marines. Yale and Haerter never hesitated. By all reports and by the recording, they never stepped back. They never shifted their weight. With their feet spread shoulder -width apart, they leaned into the danger, firing as fast as they could work their weapons. They had only one second left to live.

The truck exploded and the camera went blank. Six seconds. Not enough time to think about their families, their country, their flag, or about their lives or deaths, but more than enough time to do their duty into eternity. Two men in six seconds expressed an attitude so powerful that flight for them was not an option. Duty performed with the highest zeal imaginable saved countless lives.

****

Aunt Tita Lou would've liked Helen Keller. This Filipina woman consistently models a resilient attitude despite the painful trials she experienced. Years ago, just before her daughter delivered what would have been her grandchild, she suffered a heart attack and she and her unborn child perished. Currently another of her daughters is suffering from cancer. In her seventies, Tita runs a guest house in Los Banos, Philippines. As if it is not enough to consistently bring people into her home and feed them, she recently adopted a five-year old living on the streets near her home. While she raises this girl and runs the guest house, she cares for her brother-in-law suffering from Alzheimer's disease. She doesn't complain or feel sorry for her situation. She generously helps others. Her attitude is an inspiration to all around her.[32]

****

Earlier, I mentioned my son Bryan's brain tumor. One day I was driving back from the radiation clinic where he was going through his twice-a-day radiation treatments, and I have to admit I was a little discouraged. My vision seemed all but hopeless and the chances of our son Bryan living were bleak. From the back seat where he was sitting, Bryan piped up, "It's okay daddy, God will take care of it!" I got chills as I turned my head

> **"It's okay, daddy, God will take care of it."**

to look at him. My son was not yet four years old. How did he do that?

Attitude. Bryan recognized something at the age of three many adults would have completely missed. I needed cheering up. Instead of feeling sorry for himself, he cared about me. Today Bryan is our living miracle. You can read more about his story in *something to think about...in Reveration.*[33]

When family, friends, or co-workers use words like, "don't, can't, or won't," if you know in your heart that you are supposed to press on, push ahead! Quietly with the firmest of resolve move forward despite the obstacles!

CHAPTER FIVE

CONDUCT
The Ring Finger

Conduct influences the
behavior of leadership.

Core values posted on the wall of Veckton-Dickinson and Company—"We treat each other with respect. We do what is right. We always seek to improve. We accept personal responsibility."[34]

Conduct is the manner in which we behave. As such it influences the behavior of leadership and, in reality, validates its character. While character is about *being*, and attitude is about *motivation*, conduct is about *doing*. It is like the tip of an iceberg; it is what shows publically, but character and attitude are its foundation. Strong leaders understand that the goal of conduct is *respect* and its fruit—loyalty and esteem. Exemplary conduct is all about treating others the way we want to be treated—the Golden Rule.

It would seem that conduct today is devalued with each passing year. As our society shies away from protecting absolutes, behavior veers towards what is immoral and self-centered. Those who dare to criticize what they sincerely believe to be wrong are labeled as intolerant and marginalized as fools. Honoring others is seldom taught or emphasized. The application of kindness is meanly buried beneath the ever growing roar of a petulant, me-first society.

Respect starts early when we teach our children to rise when an older person comes into the room and to listen attentively when others talk. Respect means valuing others. It is recognition that we can learn and profit from those around us. It is a quality that builds trust and confidence in a team and organization because people sense they are valued.

Respect means thinking before we speak lest our words cause damage. When we are angry or emotionally charged, if we are not careful, we can harm the very people we love or value. Conduct involves more than just *what* we communicate it is *how* we relate and respond to people. For this reason, listening is of paramount importance. Have you

When we listen with respect, we gain trust...

ever had a conversation with someone and yet felt that they were not really paying attention to what you were saying? Have you ever been with someone who pretended to be interested in you but really was engaged in other activity or distracted by other thoughts? I'm reminded of this myself when I think of my wife trying to talk to me when the television is on!

My uncle, Ralph Erickson, spent ten years serving as a grief counselor for a funeral home. While he counseled people, his own wife received care in a home for patients with Alzheimer's disease. Ralph shared with me how he learned that the best way to help people grieving was to listen to them versus trying to prescribe solutions. Weekly within the group each person would share their story. Over time he heard the same stories repeated yet watched as people found resolution for their pain. The storytellers gained credibility and found strength through relating what they experienced. Ralph found this to be a rich time in his life for helping others who were suffering.

Ralph understood the value of listening because he grew up with a dad who did not listen to him and consequently never really knew who he was. Later in his life as a Chaplain, Ralph often met with dependents of soldiers who were misbehaving as a means to gain attention from dads who basically ignored them.

From what he learned, he was able to dispense valuable insight to his own daughter. Diane worked in a hospital ward. In her ward was a very mean woman. All of the nurses avoided this angry patient and Diane was at the end of her wits trying to figure out what to do. When she called Ralph for advice, he said, "Go in and sit down with her for half an hour. Ask her if she is scared and then listen to what she has to say." Diane followed her dad's advice. Later she reported to him that the woman was so impacted by her taking the time to listen to her fears and hear her story that she transformed from the worst patient to the best patient on that floor.

How we treat people is incredibly important. When we allow people to share their stories and we listen to them with respect, we gain their trust and establish authenticity as leaders who care.

Read what other thoughtful leaders have to say about conduct:

Benjamin Disraeli: "Circumstances are beyond human control, but our conduct is in our own power."[35]

Mark Twain: "Laws control the lesser man... Right conduct controls the greater one."[36]

Walter Lippmann: "A man has honor if he holds himself to an ideal of conduct though it is inconvenient, unprofitable, or dangerous to do so."[37]

Thomas Paine: "'Tis the business of little minds to shrink, but he whose heart is firm, and whose conscience approves his conduct, will pursue his principles unto death."[38]

Tiberius: "Let them hate me, provided they respect my conduct."[39]

Alexander the Great: "Remember upon the conduct of each depends the fate of all."[40]

When it comes to leadership, talk alone is cheap. It is action that gives words meaning. If we want people to follow our vision, we have to demonstrate that we care about them. When people see that our conduct is worthy of emulating, they will be far more likely to improve their own behavior. Noble conduct in the final analysis is sacrificial. The ne plus ultra (the ultimate) for conduct is the willingness to die for those we serve.

"Do unto others..."

****

My West Point classmate, Bill York, (a distant cousin), as a young lieutenant served with an air defense unit in Germany. On one occasion they were training in the largest maneuver area in Germany called Hohenfels. The ground was muddy and for reasons unexplained to him, they had to extend their time in the field an extra two days. To fill the time, Bill set up armor recognition classes in a tent. Unfortunately, the soldiers kept falling asleep during his class which was quite frustrating! So Bill went out and found a tear gas canister. He came back into the tent, and, in front of all the students pulled out the safety pin. Then he handed the canister to a soldier in the front row and told him and his two adjacent mates to keep awake. If the soldier let go of the spindle, the grenade would release the gas.

The soldiers kept falling asleep...

As one could imagine, for two whole classes this technique worked quite well. But during the third class, the unlucky soldier picked to hold the canister, succumbed to heavy eyelids and dropped the grenade. Immediately the spindle popped free causing a fast expulsion of CS gas into the tent. Every soldier was now awake and with reckless abandon, choking coughs, and flailing arms made their escape. Poor Bill had to find the canister and get it out or it would render their tent useless. Naturally, this meant he got the worst of the tear gas!

Bill's ability to think of creative solutions to ordinary problems suits him well. Today he runs his own business as a headhunter (not a cannibal!). Bill helps those who are looking for jobs find employment. When Daniel, a junior officer, was wounded and paralyzed from the chest down in Iraq, several academy graduates and classmates called on Bill to see if he could help this wounded warrior find work. Bill visited him at the Veteran's Hospital in Houston. He noticed that Daniel's arms were caked with dried blood and asked him what in the world happened. Daniel's wife explained that he had been playing wheel chair basketball. He was so competitive that despite his condition he spent hours competing from his wheel chair. Because he had no control of his abdominal muscles, when Daniel tried to shoot the ball he would fall out of the wheel chair thus scraping his arms so badly they bled.

By understanding the temperament and amazing attitude of this young warrior, Bill put his networking skills to work and not only landed a great job for Daniel working as a Oil & Gas Trader, he also managed through some innovative friends to score him a Toyota 4Runner specially equipped so Dan could drive it.

Eating dinner with Bill is a great adventure. The man is full of stories and while that may not be so unusual, what comes through loud and clear is his clear love for people. The fact that Bill is a successful businessman is no surprise. Consider his background: He was recruited to West Point to play football. While at the academy he played four sports. Bill loved competing. To him, the journey was just as fun as the outcome. When he left the Army after five years, he joined a small computer company in Houston at the perfect time and rode with it as it grew astronomically. He joined another small North Carolina bank that soon became the largest bank in the US (Bank of America).

Handsome, popular and cocky, Bill was used to winning and to living life to the fullest. So why didn't he become like so many people I have met through the years who when blessed with success become prideful and disdainful of those around them with lesser skills? I did not ask him this question. What I know is that he lost one of his best friends and a fellow classmate, to a horrible helicopter crash. I know he has seen the effect of pain and misfortune on the lives of those who are friends. I know that he recognized in his own life that he had become spiritually stagnant and was just "going through the motions." Pain and suffering have a way of bringing life into sharper focus.

In the great journey of life, Bill recognized that what was most important was not that he could outperform most people but rather that he could lift up those who were in need. Instead of focusing on his own desires and concerns, he has made it his passion to help others. He genuinely cares for people. Watching him at work in his office, it is obvious he has a gift for making everyone around him better. In short, Bill is a beloved man because he is a loving man. Excellent conduct left to itself may bring success, but excellent conduct with care for others creates a legacy.

****

While serving as the Commander of the 104th Division, I was blessed to have three outstanding Brigade Commanders. One of them, David Francavilla, is one of the most generous men I have ever met. He possesses an uncanny ability both to give and to bring out the best in those he leads. I believe much of this can be attributed to his behavior. There is a key reason why David builds up all those around him. Fortunately, for us, he shared with me his story. Early in his life he learned a powerful lesson about how to treat people. As a senior in high school, David was courted by several well known universities to play football. Even Notre Dame, the number one rated school in the nation at the time, expressed a strong interest in recruiting him. It felt good to be courted by schools that wrote letters, called him at home, and treated him and his family to dinners. Soon his chest and head were massively swollen with pride.

Instead of focusing on his desires, he's made it his passion to help others.

A small Christian school with only about 1,000 students called David. The coach wanted to take him to dinner. The college had a good academic reputation but its football team was at best average and unknown. David was not interested in playing for them. He remembers telling his dad that his high school team was better than their college team and that his graduating class was larger than their whole school and he was going to let their coach know these things. The arrogant words that flowed from his mouth soured his father's face and filled his eyes with disappointment. David's dad sat him down and they had a powerful conversation about respect, courtesy, and responsibility. He ensured that David knew that no one should be less noble, less kind, and less true for having been a fellow traveler in life.

So David met the coach and had a fun evening with a man not all that much older than he was. He almost signed a letter of intent with him that night but ultimately ended up playing for a school closer to home. In college, David found that he was not so special after all, there were a lot of big, strong, and fast guys and it was tough to get playing time. In his junior year a new defensive coordinator arrived at the school. After a hard first day of practice the team got in a line to shake the new coach's hand. As David approached him the man greeted him by name with a huge smile on his face. Incredibly, it was the same coach from the small

> **The arrogant words that flowed from his mouth soured his father's face...**

team he initially disdained. Because David did the right thing and treated this man with respect, he now had a coach who in turn valued him and made a difference in his football experience. That experience marked him. Today, David inspires those around him because he treats each person as important. His soldiers love serving with him and would follow him to any battle zone.

****

One of the dangers that leaders can succumb to is to assume their organizations are healthy because the metrics used to measure their productivity are strong. I almost learned this lesson the hard way. On a Friday evening I will never forget, I received a phone call from Doug. Doug was the Equal Opportunity officer for the Brigade I was commanding. He informed me that the battalion he was visiting was in such bad shape that if I did not get down there ASAP he was afraid it would implode. For at least fifteen minutes he shared his observations from time spent with soldiers in that battalion. I was stunned.

When I took over the Tiger Wolf Brigade, this battalion had some of the worst statistics in our Division. But in a short amount of time, their confident commander reported improvement in every weak area. In less than a year, they went from one of the bottom five units in the 104th Division to one of the top five. From everything my Command Sergeant Major and I heard they were doing quite well. So Doug's phone call was startling to say the least!

Within two weeks I was able to fly down and visit the unit. I asked the commander not to report to duty while I met with his soldiers. What I heard from their mouths was alarming. This man who appeared confident and motivated was, in fact, a tyrant. His temper, petty vindictiveness, and constant micromanaging managed to so alienate his subordinate leaders and soldiers that unless I promised to remove him from leadership they promised to leave in mass! I agonized over ways I could give their leader a second chance and hopefully salvage his career. Both of my bosses completely supported me to terminate or provide this man a second chance. In the end, his conduct and the indictments against him were too severe and I relieved him. Almost immediately the command climate improved and that unit moved forward. Conduct speaks louder than statistics.

CHAPTER SIX

WISDOM
The Little Finger

Wisdom influences the *efficacy* of leadership.

Wisdom is the lifelong application of knowledge with ability to do what is proper and right. Wisdom influences the efficacy of leadership. By efficacy we mean both the power to produce a desired effect and to give value. Strong leaders first recognize that *gaining wisdom will better enable them to understand, care for and develop those they serve.* Second, *wisdom equips them for solving problems, optimizing resources and overcoming those challenges which can cripple or undermine organizations.* Third, *wisdom ensures the moral compass remains on "true north."* By knowing and doing what is just and right, strong leaders possess an incalculable worth and protect their organization from moral failure even if progress is jeopardized by the preservation of truth.

Henry and Richard Blackabee in their book *Spiritual Leadership* wrote, "the best thing leaders can do for their organization is to grow personally."[41] Are you a learner? Are you growing in wisdom? *One of the best things we can do for our organization is to grow personally.* If we think about it, there are all kinds of things that have happened in our lives that caused us to learn. The day we stop learning is the day we should stop leading. I hope that day never comes in my life or your life!

Spiritual exercise is an essential ingredient which directly impacts each of the six elements. I include it in this section because of its natural fit. I have a personal goal to read at least two books every month. Part of the reason for this goal is to grow personally, because if I am going to be a commander with a great vision, I must be a learner! What good is a leader who quits learning? I will tell you that a leader who quits learning is dangerous! Conversely, you can usually trust and look up to someone who is teachable.

Beyond reading from a variety of topics, each year I make it a practice to read my Bible every day. I don't do this because I have to (legalism) but because I want to (relationship). I find that the Bible is amazingly relevant to life, provocative, and it gives me wisdom, hope, people to emulate, and solutions to all of life's challenges. The Bible is the world's all-time best seller for a reason. It contains powerful and effectual truths that are transformational. The more I learn about God and people, the more I see my own shortcomings and the need for His help with my character. When I don't exercise spiritually, my attitude lags and I am more likely to be irritable towards those I care most about which means my conduct is questionable!

If I had to pick the single most important tool for building strong leaders, I'd select spiritual exercise for the purpose of gaining wisdom. Certainly, in my life nothing else comes close in making so great a contribution. But you'll have to decide for yourself what you believe to be most important. The key is to establish a habit or pattern that will enable you to consistently learn and make prudent application with what you have learned.

Here are thoughts others leaders have to share about learning!

Abraham Lincoln: "I have been driven many times to my knees by the overwhelming conviction that I had nowhere else to go. My own wisdom, and that of all about me, seemed insufficient for the day."[42]

Thomas a Kempis: "Who is so wise as to have a perfect knowledge of all things? Therefore trust not too much to thine own opinion, but be ready also to hear the opinion of others."

Carl George: "If a group focuses on doing and deciding and fails to blend in loving and learning, its people's behavior will fall apart. They'll radiate everything but care."

Chip Heath and Dan Heath: "The growth mindset, then, is a buffer against defeatism. It reframes failure as a natural part of the change process. And that's critical, because people will persevere only if they perceive falling down as *learning* rather than *failing*."[43]

Friedrich Nietzsche: "The increase in wisdom can be measured precisely by the decrease in bile."[44]

Piet Hein: "The road to wisdom?—Well, it's plain and simple to express: Err and err and err again but less and less and less."[45]

Dan Allender: "Most real learning comes through stories."

If you are a parent, you probably have already figured out that the best way to teach your children lessons that will help them live wisely is by reading or telling them stories. I am fairly confident that when you were a child you loved hearing stories. It is amazing to me the great wealth of learning that we can amass just listening to the stories of those who went before us and those living in our midst.

****

Melissa is a wonderful mom with three very active boys! I've always been impressed with her calmness in dealing with stress or the unexpected surprises that come from parenting. When her twin sons David and Alex were about four years old, they would observe their mom driving from their car seats in the back. Melissa turned into a Type A competitive and intense woman behind a steering wheel. When other drivers would unexpectedly cut her off or drive in a way that impeded her, she would call them *idiots* and get flustered.

David and Alex picked up on her habit and soon began to call each other idiots or others that they observed. Realizing that this was not behavior she wanted duplicated she resolved to stop using the term. One day, someone again cut her off. This time, instead of using that forbidden word, she grumbled with more of a grrrr. One of the boys then asked her, "Mom was that an idiot!"

Language and how we use it makes for lots of learning opportunities. When we speak unwisely who knows who may pick up and duplicate what we wish went unsaid. Learning leaders are careful about what they say!

****

Juan is a policeman and the Command Sergeant Major of the 104th Division. On a road trip from Houston to College Station, he wistfully recounted the great road trips his family made across the United States while he was growing up. His father was a self-employed truck driver and on occasion he would tell the kids to pack up and jump in the back of their camper. He would not tell them their destination and that added to their sense of adventure. From their starting point in Warden, Washington, they drove across country. On one such trip, his dad stopped at a gas station somewhere deep in Texas.

> "Most real learning comes through stories."

After fueling he told the kids to jump in the camper and then off they went. Little Juan did not see his mother in the front and she certainly was not with them in the back. So he banged on the window to his dad who, annoyed at the interruption, asked what he wanted. His dad could not hear through the thick window so Juan did his best mouthing the words, "Where's Mom?" His dad thought he was asking where they were going and since that was always a well-guarded secret, told him to quit bothering him. Figuring his dad must know what he was doing, Juan went back to playing with his siblings in the back.

"You left your wife at the gas station!"

Fifty miles later, a Texas state trooper pulled them over. Casually he walked up to the cab and asked Juan's dad if he was missing something. When his father gave the officer a puzzled look, the trooper said, "You left your wife at the gas station!" Of course Juan's mom's version was much better. She saw her husband driving off without her and ran down the road chasing the camper and yelling at him to stop! He never saw her. He made the assumption she was in the back with the kids. And from that great adventure, Juan learned a life lesson. Be careful about making assumptions!

****

Lieutenant General (Ret) Sam Wilson is a profound example of a learning leader. Sam grew up on a 150 acre farm in rural Virginia. His parents were readers, and they fostered in their children a deep love of books. Sam's mother, a former public school teacher, insisted that his older sister and three brothers value learning. She taught them much about discipline, self-control, and how to think logically. Meanwhile, Sam's father was a prolific storyteller. His imagination and ability to turn everyday events and circumstances into stories taught Sam to be observant and creative. By consistently studying, reading and keeping up with current events, it was amazing what he accomplished.

At the young age of sixteen, Sam joined the Virginia National Guard. His leadership skills were such that he was sent to the Infantry Officer Candidate School (OCS). Sam graduated at the head of his class and upon his promotion to Second Lieutenant he was selected to teach at the Infantry School. By the age of nineteen he was teaching counter-insurgency. President Roosevelt asked for volunteers for a dangerous mission and Sam was selected. He was one of Merrill's Marauders in WWII serving behind enemy lines in Burma.

In September 1947, Sam entered the Army's Foreign Area Specialist Training Program (FASTP) and was enrolled in graduate school at Columbia University. From there he went on to become virtually fluent in Russian with a good grasp of many other languages. What makes him special is not just that he personally amassed knowledge but that he has a knack for making any organization he serves better. His innovative insight and pursuit of excellence led to his selection to the Army Infantry Hall of Fame, US Military Intelligence Hall of Fame, Army Ranger Hall of Fame, and the Defense Intelligence Agency US Attaché Hall of Fame. General Wilson was also named Professor Emeritus for the Army John F. Kennedy Special Warfare Center & School and awarded the State of Virginia Cultural Laureate for Public Service by Virginia Cultural Laureate Foundation. He was the 1994 winner and first recipient of the General Doolittle Educator of the Year Award for distinguished service to Special Operations Education.[46]

General Wilson despite never attaining a college degree became President of Hampden-Sydney College and in 2000 he was named President Emeritus. When I emailed LTG (ret) Jerry Boykin and asked if he had someone he could suggest as an example to us of a leader of wisdom, he quickly suggested Sam Wilson.

In describing him he wrote: "He is a lifelong learner who at 87 years old still teaches and studies myriad subjects. When you sit and talk to him, he is conversant on many subjects and can discuss them in fluent Russian. His continual grasp of current events is impressive and he puts things in the context of history."

****

Doug was the pastor of a church in Arizona. With his spouse and two sons everything seemed wonderful. One night his wife did not come home. He went out looking for her and found her with the man who was his key helper in the church. He was devastated and did not know what to do. He lay on the floor of his home for days crying. After his wife left him, his life descended into chaos. For several years he tried to make things work but to no avail. Finally, he found church homes for all the folks in his congregation, closed the church and left the ministry with a broken heart. Despite the fact that it was his wife who was unfaithful, *he* felt he had let people down. Frustrated, angry with God, confused and depressed, one day he decided to just walk out into the desert and die.

Without telling his sons Bryan and Matthew, Doug walked far into the Arizona wilderness. After several days, he was overcome by the heat and became so dehydrated he could not even walk. He was ready to die yet rationalized that he was not committing suicide because the elements would overtake him. Doug lay on prominent ground and positioned himself so searchers could easily find his body. He didn't want to be eaten by some varmint. He folded his arms on his chest and closed his eyes. All of sudden he felt something tap him. Repeatedly he was touched and he opened his eyes. All around he saw blue sky yet directly above him was a rain cloud. Heavy drops fell on him which he gulped down and then filled the containers he had with him. He was revived!

Two nights later Doug verbally exploded calling God every filthy word he could think and hurling accusation upon accusation. For what seemed like hours he ranted, screamed, and cussed at God for all his problems. Then he just stopped. In that moment, he experienced a great release. For the first time in a long time, he heard the voice of God speak to him. Ashamed of his words, he expected to be struck by a lightning bolt; instead, he heard God say, "This isn't news to Me, you've had this in your heart all along. Now that you've gotten it out I can begin to heal you."

Incredibly Doug survived for ten months in that desert. Fortunately, he was somewhat of a survivalist with firsthand experience in how to live in a desert environment. Now you might wonder what in the world does this story have to do with wisdom? In a profound sense, when Doug was stripped of everything that mattered and left with lots of time to think, his ability to learn was actually heightened. During this period he established with God a relationship he didn't previously think was possible. Drawing from his memories of the Bible and from uninterrupted time to reflect, Doug began to understand how much God cared for him. In the wilderness he discovered his Father's love.

This broken pastor realized that there were so many people like him, who were hurting and needed help—not just someone to say, "I'll pray for you," but to actually care. One night while sitting by a fire, he heard a voice say "536-9325." Several times that number was repeated. He remembered it was the number of a church where he had once served.

He was ready to die...

Doug walked out of the desert to a payphone and called that number. He asked for the pastor and was told he no longer ministered there. Finding out his new number, Doug made a collect call and connected with his former pastor, Raymond. He told him his location and shared he was ready to do whatever God wanted for him next. His relation had been built on material things, his family, and things that were temporal. Now that his relationship with God was renewed he knew he needed to help hurting people.

In order to start afresh, Doug returned to Lawton, Oklahoma where his parents lived. In their church, the first person he encountered was Bill, a longtime friend, and the state founder and director of Teen Challenge. Bill invited Doug to come and work with him. With a grateful heart he accepted and began a ministry to hurting teens.

Wisdom is often born through pain...

Bryan and Matthew were reunited and reconciled with their father. Not a day passes by without Doug remembering the grace God extended to him. When I spoke with him, he shared how blessed he was to be remarried to Carolyn—a fantastic wife and friend! "Promises have to die before they can be fulfilled."

Wisdom is often born through pain. She is nurtured by suffering and matured through grief. Likewise, amassing wisdom can lead to both vexation and sorrow. The wise King Solomon noted, "For with much wisdom is much sorrow; as knowledge increases, grief increases."[47] Leaders who are able to gain knowledge through adversity bring incalculable worth to their organizations. Life does not always go the way we expect. When we are able to learn from our mistakes, the twists and turns of fate, and the actions of good and bad people, we possess the power to discern and to dispense insight.

CHAPTER SEVEN

THE LEADER
Putting the Hand to Work!

Definition of a Leader:
A leader is a person people reliably follow to a place they wouldn't normally go.

"The hand is the artisan of the soul. It is the second member of the human trinity of head and hand and heart. A man has no faculty more human that his hand, none more beautiful nor expressive nor productive"—Robert Leckie in *Helmet For My Pillow*

Strong leaders are selective and deliberate about what they put their hands to and the manner in which they operate them. They not only effectively utilize the six essential elements, they also understand the appropriate style of leadership to execute within their organization. This is where wisdom and discernment are of particular importance. When this phenomenon occurs we have a condition that is transformational!

Transformational Leadership = Leadership which effectively combines all six elements (vision, teamwork, character, attitude, conduct and wisdom) **with the appropriate style so as to lead an organization to sustained success.**

Strong leaders recognize leadership styles are tailored to meet—at a minimum—three levels people possess in every organization: skill, ownership and focus. It is unwise for a leader to lock in on one leadership style and operate only in that style because conditions may warrant a different approach. It is important also to understand that leaders themselves require a maturation process. One style does not fit all circumstances or environments. Before determining which method to use, the strong leader is wise to understand the skill, ownership and focus level of those whom he or she is serving.

Skill Level—the less proficient a worker's skill level is the more directive the leadership style will be.

Proficiency—Low (LP); Moderate (MP); High (HP)

Ownership Level—by ownership we mean an employee's investment in an organization's vision, mission, goals and requirements. Generally the less committed an employee, the more directive the leader must be.

Commitment—Low (LC); Moderate (MC); High (HC)

Focus Level—generally the more immature a person, the more self-oriented he or she will be. As people mature they tend to become more aware of the needs and concerns of their teammates. While a person will always have personal needs, the individual who serves for the good of the team will in the end be most constructive towards team success and harmony. In organizations where self-orientation is high, a more directive style of leadership is necessary.

Focus—Self Oriented (SO); Team Oriented (TO)

Young leaders will not necessarily have the experience and maturity to coach, support or empower followers. For example, a new or inexperienced leader would face ridicule or resentment if he tried to coach an experienced veteran. Early on, the leader provides the directives the organization stipulates and ensures that rules and processes are followed. In time as the leader learns how the organization operates, he should become more participatory. Change is a constant with every organization that experiences employee turnover. A mature organization gaining new employees will require directive leadership combined with supportive or empowering leadership.

After studying the model on the next page, we will ask you questions to consider for each style. In essence, our hope is that our questions will stimulate helpful interaction and reflection regarding style implementation! The answers or conclusions you reach will be situation-dependent. This in turn calls for wisdom in that it would be easy to become prescriptive with solutions to contrasting work and employee challenges—just be careful. Sometimes even methods which seem counterintuitive work simply because the leader's hand was genuinely engaged with all the essential elements at work![48]

Transformational Leadership

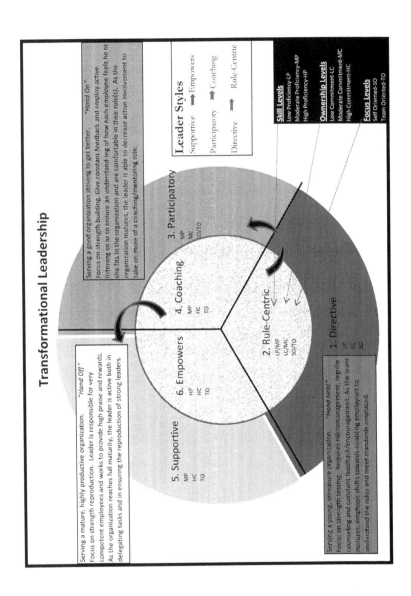

Serving a mature, highly productive organization. *"Hand Off"* Focus on strength reproduction. Leader is responsible for very competent employees and works to provide high praise and rewards. As the organization reaches full maturity, the leader is active both in delegating tasks and in ensuring the reproduction of strong leaders.

Serving a good organization striving to get better. *"Hand On"* Focus on strength building. Give constant feedback and employ active listening so as to ensure an understand-ing of how each employee feels he or she fits in the organization and are comfortable in their role(s). As the organization matures, the leader is able to decrease active involvement to take on more of a coaching/mentoring role.

Serving a young, immature organization. *"Hand Held"* Focus on strength testing. Requires micromanagement, regular counseling and constant feedback/encouragement. As the team matures, emphasis shift towards enabling employees to understand the rules and meet standards emplaced.

Leader Styles

Supportive ➡ Empowers

Participatory ➡ Coaching

Directive ➡ Rule-Centric

Skill Levels
Low Proficiency-LP
Moderate Proficiency-MP
High Proficiency-HP

Ownership Levels
Low Commitment-LC
Moderate Commitment-MC
High Commitment-HC

Focus Levels
Self Oriented-SO
Team Oriented-TO

3. Participatory
MP
MC
SO/TO

4. Coaching
MP
HC
TO

5. Supportive
MP
HC
TO

6. Empowers
HP
HC
TO

2. Rule-Centric
LP/MP
LC/MC
SO/TO

1. Directive
LP
LC
SO

The Directive, Rule Centric Leader

Key Questions:

1. What are the indicators within an organization that a directive, rules emphasis approach is no longer effective?

2. What often happens when a leader remains overly focused on micromanaging or controlling people and systems?

3. High absenteeism and low morale may indicate employee dissatisfaction with the leader or work environment. How might this problem be addressed?

4. How should a leader lead an organization with a mixture of immature, mature, self oriented and team oriented employees that are underachieving?

5. What are effective ways for the leader to test for employee strengths?

6. How does a rule-centric approach actually enhance the leader's ability to lead?

7. How does the leader know when it is safe to become more participatory ?

Beware with the directive method of becoming heavy handed, overly controlling (which may be a sign of insecurity), or so dictatorial that followers become intimidated, resentful or disinclined to work.

The Participatory-Coaching Leader

Key Questions:

1. What are the indicators within an organization that a participatory, coaching approach is no longer effective?

2. What are the dangers of a leader remaining overly focused on working within the team and coaching?

3. What are effective ways for the leader to build employee strengths and mitigate weaknesses?

4 When quality is more important than speed and time is available for the leader to invest in participating and coaching, what tangible benefits ensue?

5. What are potential obstacles that might hinder the leader from investing the time necessary to develop employee strengths?

6. What kind of activities might the coach employ to strengthen teamwork?

The Supportive-Empowering Leader

Key Questions:

1. What are the indicators within an organization that a supportive, empowering approach is no longer effective?

2. What may happen if the leader is too prone to delegate tasks and responsibilities?

3. What are effective ways for the leader to reproduce strong leaders?

4. What should the goal be for every strong leader with respect to reproduction?

****

On three different occasions my job was to start a new church. In each case I started with small core teams and directive leadership was necessary because everyone who volunteered to join the team needed to know their respective responsibilities and the guidelines which would help us succeed. Because in most cases I was working with experienced adults, it only took about six months to transition to participatory leadership. As a group we designed and passed out flyers to alert the community to our presence and vision. We brainstormed ideas for serving the people in our neighborhoods. We had lots of fun welcoming and serving new attendees.

After about a year, it was possible for me to focus on my responsibilities in teaching and leading music, while coaching the other leaders. While each church grew and I served with wonderful people, I was never able to move to a supportive or empowering leadership style. The first church ended up merging with another church while the two succeeding churches both eventually died.

In a new church, many people come who are needy and require much counseling and support. To prepare for this, it is essential that there is either a large and healthy core group or the ability to bring in strong trainers. The former can usually absorb and naturally help those who are needy while the latter is able to bring training that brings those in need to a position of health (or referral to another church). Leaders who are strong trainers or builders are excellent at creating structure within an organization that moves people from close direction to the place where they eventually are empowered to themselves become leaders.

Four of my personal strengths fit well in entrepreneurial work—activator, ideation, positivity and strategic.[49] My fifth strength is maximizing which is comical. In essence, I function best when an organization needs to go from good to great. This is probably a strong reason why I thrive within the military. I have always had a group that is trained and merely needs to move to the next level. Unfortunately, with new churches there is often a need to grow from raw to great—a long progression that requires leaders who are methodical builders and have the necessary time to devote. I am not an effective trainer/builder. Without a large core group or the necessary trainers and builders, I could not just coach the core team. By default, I also needed to train those who were new and joined our team—something for which I wasn't well suited.

Why do I share this? In many ways, the churches I started mirror the challenges business or other nonprofit organizations face. It is important for you to understand your own strengths and limitations so you not only master the six essential elements but also have a sane appreciation of what styles of leadership best fit your personality and gifting. Don't try to do what you are not best suited for or you may become frustrated and in turn frustrate those around you.

Had I known twenty years ago what I know now I would not have become a church planter. I would have looked for healthy churches already established looking to grow to the next level. Because I love to create, think strategically, initiate new projects, and encourage others, running my own nonprofit First Cause is rewarding. I am able to maximize our team's work and help other organizations develop their leaders. The tool that helped me identify my strengths is called StrengthsFinder 2.0 by Tom Rath. I strongly recommend you purchase the book and take the test online to identify your five strengths. You can find the order information at: www.strengthsfinder.com. Happy hunting!

****

The strong leader's hand is most effective when it is used in the proper context with the right method and perspective. I suspect this will never be easy! I say this because despite decades of leadership experience, I am often reminded of how easy it is to come up short as a leader. While still in high school, my youngest son Stephen and I were engaged in a very competitive game of basketball. The score was close when we got into a disagreement and by force of will, my opinion prevailed. Stephen's spirit changed and he quit competing. Eventually, he just walked away and went inside the house. I felt like he quit for no good reason and so I followed him asking him what the matter was. He wouldn't answer me and just continued down the stairs to his room.

Concerned by his demeanor, I followed him into his room and pressed him for an answer. He looked me in the eye but would not reply. Finally, after assuring him that I truly wanted to know what was in his heart he responded. "Dad, you're always right." And then I understood the problem. At that critical point I had a significant choice to make. I could say "No, I'm not always right." and by doing so validate his observation for I would be correcting him again. I could argue my case for why I thought my call on the court was correct and in the process further quench his spirit. Or I could humble myself and recognize the accuracy of his statement. I chose the latter. I apologized to him for not accepting his version of what happened during the game. I told him I loved him and it was more important to me to have his respect and to know that I listened and valued his opinion than for me to get my way.

Strong leaders will fail. They will make mistakes and say or do things that should not be said or done. I know—I have made my share of mistakes and regret things I have done that came from a hasty hand. I hope that you will take what I have learned and improve upon it. Leading is a great privilege. It is an adventure that I hope you will have opportunity to undertake whether it is in your home, in your community, at work, or at play. Right now, my hand is in the form of a salute—to you! I can't wait to hear your stories!

Six Essential Elements Review

Vision: Influences the *direction* and *commitment* of leadership.

◊ Four important facets related to vision:

☐ *First, it is crucial we craft a vision that is sound and enduring.*

☐ *Second, we have to effectively communicate it.*

☐ *Third, we have to obtain buy-in.*

☐ *Fourth, we must hold it with an open hand.*

Teamwork: Influences the *magnitude* of leadership.

◊ First, leaders must lead their team in modeling vulnerability.

◊ Second, strong leaders overcome team members fear of conflict by demonstrating the ability to both allow for disagreement and to teach their subordinates or peers that decision-making is actually improved be inviting dissenting views.

◊ Third, strong leaders erase a lack of commitment by team members by holding to goals and established standards.

◊ Fourth, strong leaders tackle head first difficult issues.

◊ Fifth, strong leaders "focus on collective outcomes."

◊ Sixth, strong leaders work hard at building and

sustaining solid relationships.

Character: Influences the *nature* and *quality* of leadership.
◊ Trust is an essential part of character.
◊ Rest is crucial for maintaining our character.

Attitude: Influences the *spirit*, *will* and *force* of leadership.
◊ Humility is a key virtue in effecting our attitude.
◊ Humor is a wonderful technique for dissolving bad attitudes.
◊ Physical exercise is indispensable in maintaining a healthy attitude.

Conduct: Influences the *behavior* of leadership.
◊ Remember the *Golden Rule*!
◊ Respect is a key attribute in how we treat people.
   □ *Listening to people is an important part of respect.*

Wisdom: Influences the *efficacy* of leadership.
◊ One of the best things we can do for our organization is to grow personally.
   □ *Wisdom better enables leaders to understand, care for, and develop those they serve.*
   □ *Wisdom equips leaders for solving problems, optimizing resources, and overcoming those challenges which can*

cripple or undermine organizations.

☐ *Wisdom ensures the moral compass remains on "true north."*

◊ Spiritual exercise is vital for leaders in wisdom, vision, character, attitude and conduct development.

◊ Story telling is one of the most effective ways to help people learn!

Endnotes

[1]The plural term we is used because I am indebted to others who helped me with this work—Dr. John George, LTG (retired) Don Parker, Greg Hiebert, Mark Entner, Will Robertson and the countless audiences with whom I have shared this illustration and received helpful feedback!

[2]Mark Entner, West Point class of 1983 and a keen student of leadership penned this definition after observing that the majority of books he read about leadership did not define what a leader is!

[3]http://dictionary.reference.com/browse/strong.

[4]Rushworth M. Kidder, *How Good People Make Tough Choices* (New York, 1995) 101.

Vision

[5]http://www.quoteworld.org/quotes/975.

[6]http://quoteworld.org/quotes/1220.

[7]George Barna, *The Power of Vision*, (Ventura, CA), 47.

[8]http://news.yahoo.com/s/ap/20110406/ap_on_re_as/as_japan_earthquake_warnings_in_stone.

[9]Ibid.

[10]Gerald Astor, *Terrible Terry Allen*, (New York).

Teamwork

[11]http://www.tablegroup.com/books/dysfunctions/the_five_dysfunctions.pdf. The five points come from Patrick Lencioni's book The Five Dysfunctions of a Team. I have preserved the points but amplified upon them with personal thoughts.

[12]http://www.icelebz.com/quotes/mike_krzyzewski/.

[13]http://www.brainyquote.com/quotes/quotes/v/vincelomba151259.html.

Character

[14]Contributed by Greg Hiebert, my West Point classmate and brother of Donald Hiebert.

[15]http://thinkexist.com/quotation/
character_may_almost_be_called_the_most_effective/154739.html.

[16]http://www.quotedb.com/quotes/1277.

[17]http://www.quotationspage.com/quote/29760.html.

[18]http://quoteworld.org/quotes/7543

[19]http://www.brainyquote.com/quotes/quotes/b/
billygraha161989.html.

[20]Rushworth M. Kidder, *How Good People Make Tough Choices*, (New York, 1995), 54.

[21]Ibid, 54,55.

[22]Ibid, 55.

[23]Chip Heath & Dan Heath, Switch, (Broadway Books New York, 2010), 10.

[24]Contributed by Daniel Breckel.

Attitude

[25]Oliver L. North and FOX News Channel, *American Heroes*, (Nashville, TN, 2009), 148.

[26]http://www.brainyquote.com/quotes/keywords/humility_6.html.

[27]http://www.marshallfoundation.org/MarshallonLeadership.htm.

[28]http://thinkexist.com/quotes/charles_r._swindoll/.

[29]http://www.career-success-for-newbies.com/attitude-quotes.html.

[30]http://en.wikiquote.org/wiki/F._Scott_Fitzgerald.

[31]Contributed by Greg Hiebert.

[32]Contributed by Barbara Ennis.

[33]To order this book, go to www.firstcause.org.

Conduct

[34]http://www.bd.com/aboutbd/values/.

[35]http://quotationsbook.com/quote/6800/#axzz1HT9lEwYl.

[36]http://thinkexist.com/quotation/laws_control_the_lesser_man-right_conduct/215710.html.

[37]http://www.brainyquote.com/quotes/authors/w/

walter_lippmann.html.

[38]http://www.quotedb.com/quotes/2707

[39]http://www.brainyquote.com/quotes/keywords/conduct_5.html.

[40]http://quotationsbook.com/quote/40290/#axzz1HT9lEwYl.

Wisdom

[41]Henry and Richard Blackaby, *Spiritual Leadership*, (Nashville, TN), 31.

[42]http://www.quotedb.com/quotes/3681.

[43]Chip Heath & Dan Heath, *Switch*, (Broadway Books, 2010), 169.

[44]Friedrich Nietzsche, *Sämtliche Werke: Kritische Studienausgabe*, vol. 2, Berlin (Berlin, 1980). 701

[45]http://quotationsbook.com/quote/26722/#axzz1HT9lEwYl.

[46]Information taken from two websites: http://en.wikipedia.org/wiki/Samuel_V._Wilson and http:// www.stevenpressfield.com/2010/07/general-sam-v-wilson/

[47]Ecclesiastes 1:18, *The Minister's Bible*, (Nashville, TN, Holman Christian Standard Bible, 2005), 869.

Putting the Hand to Work

[48]Go to http://www.mindtools.com/pages/article/newLDR_84.htm to discover a great site on leadership.

[49]These terms are defined in *STRENGTHSFINDER 2.0* by Tom Rath, (New York, 2007), 41-165.

ABOUT THE AUTHOR

No stranger to leadership, Daniel York has directed or led people for over forty years to include his current position as the Commanding General of the 104th Division (Leader Training). Growing up in Okinawa, South Korea, Japan, the Philippines, and across the U.S., he has learned much about leading in different cultures and settings.

Dan graduated from West Point in 1981 and was commissioned a Second Lieutenant in the U.S. Army. He served with the 101st Airborne (Air Assault) Division and as a company commander deployed his unit to the Middle East. In 1986 he joined the Army Reserves where he served as a commander at every level to include his most recent selection to command the 86th Division. Dan served on staff with The Navigators for ten years during which time he received a Master of Divinity from Bethel Seminary (West) in San Diego, CA before moving with his family in 1991 to Oregon to plant and pastor Horizon Community Church. In 2000, he started the nonprofit First Cause, an organization committed to developing leaders currently active in five countries. He has written five books and recorded seven albums of original music. He and his wife Kathleen have been married for over 28 years and have three children, Bryan, Sarah and Stephen.

TO SCHEDULE A
STRONG
LEADER'S HAND
EVENT

contact us at
dan@firstcause.org

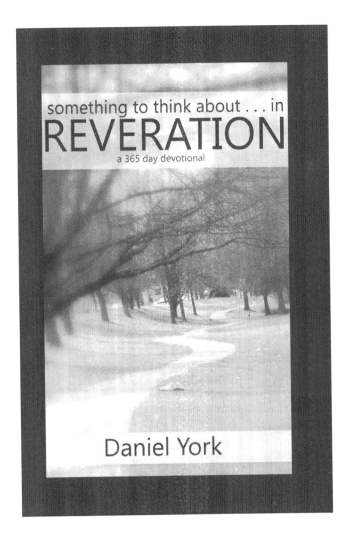

something to think about . . . in

REVERATION

a 365 day devotional

Daniel York

Available at
www.firstcause.org

THE STRONG LEADER'S HAND

6 ESSENTIAL ELEMENTS
EVERY LEADER MUST MASTER

DANIEL YORK

Order one for a friend at
www.firstcause.org

Also available at
www.firstcause.org

The newest original songs by Daniel York

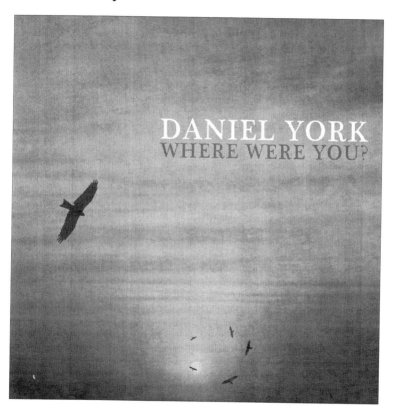

Go to
www.firstcause.org

Order your Christmas music here!

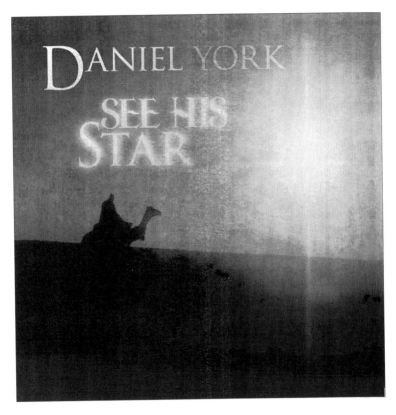

All original songs at www.firstcause.org

Songs from the heart
by Daniel York

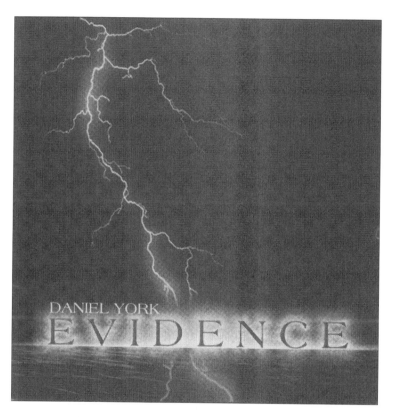

Come and listen at
www.firstcause.org

Additional leadership training
tools available online at
www.firstcause.org

We hope you enjoyed this book!
We would love to hear your
stories. Write us at
dan@firstcause.org.

Never stop learning!

Made in the USA
Lexington, KY
04 February 2012